The author wishes to thank the following
for their help and cooperation:
MERCEDES-BENZ • KING TRAILERS •
HOYNOR • ABBEY HILL • BOEING •
TEREX • PORT OF TILBURY • SCHMIDT •
CRANE FRUEHAUF • GENERAL MOTORS •
DENNIS EAGLE • VOLVO BM •
LONDON FIRE SERVICE

First U.S. edition 1992
First published in Great Britain in 1991 by Walker Books Ltd., London.

ISBN 1-56402-005-3

Library of Congress Catalog Card Number 91-71823
Library of Congress Cataloging-in-Publication Data
Radford, Derek.
Cargo machines and what they do/Derek Radford—1st U.S. ed.
p. cm.
Summary: Text and pictures introduce machines that carry things,
such as cargo planes, garbage trucks, and space vehicles.
ISBN 1-56402-005-3: $8.95
1. Machinery—Juvenile literature. 2. Cargo handling—Equipment—Juvenile literature.
[1. Cargo handling—Equipment. 2. Machinery.] I. Title.
TJ147.R28 1992   91-71823
629.04'8—dc20   CIP
                                              AC

10 9 8 7 6 5 4 3 2 1

Printed and bound in Hong Kong by Imago

Candlewick Press
2067 Massachusetts Avenue
Cambridge, Massachusetts 02140

DEREK RADFORD
CARGO MACHINES
AND WHAT THEY DO

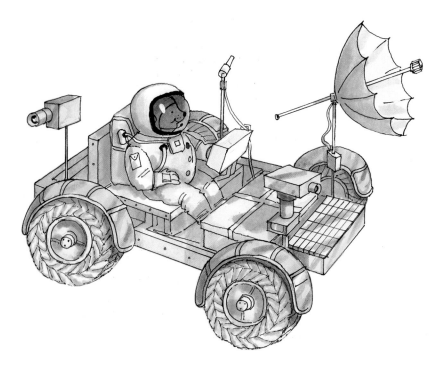

CANDLEWICK PRESS
CAMBRIDGE, MASSACHUSETTS

Cargo plane

Some airplanes carry passengers. Other planes carry only cargo. The cargo, which might be machinery, motors, food, or clothing, is packed in steel containers.

Inside the aircraft the heavy containers move on rollers.

The rear cargo door opens up.

The double-deck loader is controlled by a driver in the cab.

RATTLE RATTLE

This baggage cart takes suitcases to a passenger plane.

baggage cart

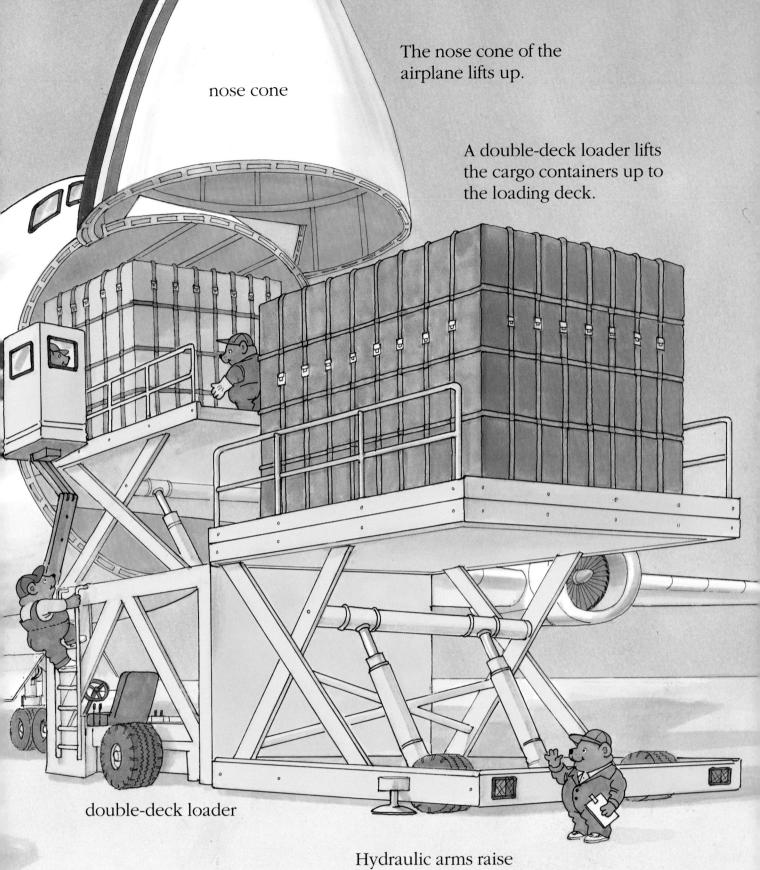

nose cone

The nose cone of the
airplane lifts up.

A double-deck loader lifts
the cargo containers up to
the loading deck.

double-deck loader

Hydraulic arms raise
and lower the double-
deck loader.

Log loader

Log loaders load big tree trunks onto trucks to be taken to the sawmills. Trees take a long time to grow, so new forests must be planted to replace the ones cut down.

Some forests are specially planted for timber and papermaking.

The driver opens and closes the jaws to pick up and stack logs.

WB/181C

BRRR!

It's cold work in the North.

This diesel truck can carry up to 26 tons.

log loader

The giant log loader has strong
mechanical jaws for lifting
and carrying heavy trunks.
It can lift up to 28 tons at once.

WB/1811

WB/1812

These logs have been
felled by chain saws.

Sea cargo

Most sea cargo – cars, food, machinery, and so on – travels in steel containers. Some containers are refrigerated.

A gantry crane lifts a container from the ship, moves it along rails, and lowers it onto the dock.

A fork-lift truck carries small loads.

A straddler lowers a container onto a truck.

A driver controls the gantry crane from this cabin.

A straddler carrier goes to pick up a container.

container

The gantry crane moves along a track.

straddler carrier

A truck waits for a straddler to bring a container.

Gasoline tanker

Gasoline is transported to garages in sealed tankers. A tanker has seven separate compartments so that it can carry different grades of gasoline.

The garage owner uses a long dipstick to check the amount of gasoline delivered.

LONG VEHICLE

LONG VEHICLE

As well as rear taillights, the tanker has rear headlights for backing up in the dark.

Hoses are stored around the tank. They can be locked together to make an extra-long hose.

CLANG!

FLAMMABLE

GARAGE

Each compartment has its own discharge valve.

The garage's underground supply tanks are usually well away from the gas pumps.

gas pump

This car has broken down.

Dump trucks

Giant dump trucks can move huge amounts of earth, stone, or sand over bumpy ground.

Controls in the cab enable the driver to tip the load in the right place.

A safety mesh protects the driver from falling rock.

hydraulic arms

The dump truck can ride over rough ground because each wheel moves independently.

Extending wing mirrors help
the driver to see when he is
backing up and tipping.

wing mirror

Big, deep-tread tires cope with
mud, sand, or jagged rocks.

RUMBLE! RUMBLE!

These dump trucks can
carry up to 38 tons.

CRUNCH!!

Car transporter

New vehicles are taken on special transporters from the factories where they are built to the showrooms and garages where they will be sold.

Each car is attached with straps. Cars at the back have their rear wheels fitted into chocks.

Loading and unloading must be done very carefully to avoid damaging the cars.

A ramp is extended for loading. Later it slides back into the transporter.

Safety bars hold
cars in place.

To make the best use
of space, some cars are
parked at an angle.

Levers raise and
lower the car decks.

The load is checked. Cars
for the first delivery must
be positioned so that they
are easy to drive off.

Trucks and trailers

When the circus is on the move, everything
is transported in giant trailers towed by
powerful trucks. "Everything" includes the
big top, the Ferris wheel, the big dipper,
bumper cars, and sideshows!

big top

CIRCUS

The trailer has support legs so
that it can stand alone if the
truck is needed elsewhere.

Smoke from the diesel engine comes out at the top of the exhaust stack.

antenna

Horns alert other drivers on the road.

A CB radio helps drivers keep in touch on long trips.

tool kit

The driver repairs the exhaust stack.

The truck has 10 wheels.
The trailer has 12 wheels.

Snow vehicles

All travel is brought to a halt when snow blocks roads, but snow cutters and blowers can clear roads in a matter of hours.

Flashing lights warn other vehicles that the snow machines are at work.

The funnels can blow snow up to 54 yards away.

The cutter breaks up packed snow and forces it out through funnels.

A snow cutter has big scoops at the front.

snow cutter

Steel chains on the cutter's wheels give them better traction.

This vehicle scatters sand on the road to make it less slippery.

WHOOSH!

The driver can move the funnels to send snow in any direction.

snow blower

A snow blower opens its gates and takes loose snow in through funnels.

Low bed

A low bed is a huge carrier used for transporting heavy or slow machines such as excavators, or equipment like boilers and furnaces.

The excavator uses its own power to crawl up a ramp onto the low bed.

excavator

low bed

The rear wheels have power steering to control the vehicle around corners.

Steel cables hold the load in place.

This low bed has 24 wheels. It can carry up to 126 tons.

The truck is articulated,
which means it is joined
to the low bed but can
move freely from side to side.

warning lights

Police officers make
sure that roads are clear.

The low bed route needs
to be carefully planned to
avoid busy or narrow roads,
low bridges, and tunnels.

Garbage truck

Each day millions of used bottles, cans, boxes, and paper are collected by garbage trucks and taken to city dumps or to recycling plants. Today we recycle paper, cans, and bottles.

A sweeper plate inside the garbage truck keeps pushing in the garbage.

sweeper plate

SWISH!

SWISH!

A street cleaner brushes and sucks up dirt.

Plastic bags and trash from trash cans are thrown into the garbage truck.

Workers wear thick overalls and gloves for protection against dirt and cuts.

Inside the garbage truck, the trash is packed down under pressure so that it takes up a smaller space.

The steel body of the garbage truck has raised ribs to give it extra strength.

DANGER
STAND
CLEAR

At the recycling plant an ejector plate inside the garbage truck pushes the trash out.

Space vehicles

Spacecraft such as Apollo 15 can travel up to 24,800 miles per hour. They are powerful enough to carry astronauts and their equipment to the moon – 236,000 miles from the earth.

The command module orbited the moon while the astronauts worked on the surface.

The lunar rover was located by signals sent out by its navigation equipment.

Batteries provided power. Top speed: 10 mph.

The lunar rover was made of lightweight metals. It weighed 458 lb on earth but only 79 lb on the moon.

Steel wire-mesh wheels gripped the surface of the moon.

lunar module

The lunar module stood on four round feet so that its power thrusters were kept clear of the moon's surface.

The lunar rover collected samples of soil and rock.

crater

Fire engine

When the alarm rings at the fire station, the crew jumps onto the engines. One engine carries water and chemical foam. The other engine carries a long, movable ladder.

The extension ladder reaches to the upstairs windows.

Police keep back the crowds.

NEE-NA-NEE-NA!

Extra water comes from a pipe under the road.

The fire chief uses a loud bullhorn to give instructions.

WHOOSH!

A powerful jet of water is directed at the flames.

Smoke is deadly, so firefighters wear oxygen masks.

An ax is used to break down doors.

oxygen